HOW **STEM** BUILT THE
CHINESE DYNASTIES

MICHAEL HESSEL-MIAL

Rosen
YA

New York

Published in 2020 by The Rosen Publishing Group, Inc.
29 East 21st Street, New York, NY 10010

Library of Congress Cataloging-in-Publication Data

Names: Hessel-Mial, Michael, author.
Title: How STEM built the Chinese dynasties / Michael Hessel-Mial.
Description: First edition. | New York : Rosen Publishing, 2020. | Series: How STEM built empires | Audience: Grades: 7 to 12. | Includes bibliographical references and index.
Identifiers: LCCN 2019008455| ISBN 9781725341388 (library bound) | ISBN 9781725341371 (pbk.)
Subjects: LCSH: Science—China—History—Juvenile literature. | Technology—China—History—Juvenile literature. | Engineering—China—History—Juvenile literature. | Mathematics—China—History—Juvenile literature. | China—Civilization—Juvenile literature.
Classification: LCC Q127.C5 H597 2020 | DDC 303.48/30951—dc23
LC record available at https://lccn.loc.gov/2019008455

Manufactured in China

On the cover: The Great Wall of China was built on a foundation of other incredible Chinese STEM knowledge.

CONTENTS

INTRODUCTION

I n the early 1900s, China was stagnating. Empires like Japan and England had taken control of parts of the country after several humiliating wars, and countless peasants were on the brink of starvation. Many observers complained that the Chinese were too tied to their traditions to advance in the modern world. Some argued that people needed to stop following the old ways—and start embracing modern scientific ideas—to develop the country. People listened. Today, China is one of the fastest-growing economies in the world and is entering the realm of world superpower.

Is this recent rise a new development? Is China late to the game, only becoming successful after abandoning its past? Not quite. In fact, the Central Kingdom (the official name of Imperial China) was perhaps the most enduring power in world history. When Italian merchant Marco Polo visited China in the late thirteenth century, he was stunned by what he saw: innovations such as paper money and the use of coal as fuel, unheard of in Europe at the time, were commonplace in China. For centuries after, China was admired by the rest of the world for its million-person cities, vast naval power, and stunning inventions. Indeed, China's four great inventions (gunpowder, paper, printing, and the compass) alone would change

the course of science, technology, engineering, and math (STEM).

The story of Imperial China is a gripping drama of competing states and dynasties, with periods of flourishing culture alternating with sudden shifts in power. Traditional Chinese historians believed in the Mandate of Heaven, which declared that the right to rule China was chosen by cosmic destiny—a concept with major political, religious, and scientific consequences.

Chinese STEM, like that of other empires, was shaped by values and beliefs specific to China. Astronomy stemmed from a desire to predict the dynasty's future, which eventually paved the way for advancements in mechanical engineering and mathematics. Religious beliefs in the mystical laws of nature led to explorations of chemical properties and the workings of the human body. Understanding these cultural values is vital to understanding the STEM they eventually shaped.

It is common to think of the history of STEM as a succession of great names, moving in a direct line from Archimedes to Isaac Newton to Albert Einstein. China itself offers many talented figures who contributed to STEM, but these thinkers, scientists, and inventors are just part of the story. Many of China's inventions evolved over long time periods, spread by diffusion, and were anonymously perfected over time.

As China's fortunes rose and fell through the centuries, geniuses in science, politics, and warfare would toil alongside unknown inventors and workers solving problems. People would debate the most virtuous way to run a state or simply seize it outright. People discussed the citizen's role in the country, China's place in the world, and the natural world's place in the cosmos. Each of these questions spurred people to discover and innovate with STEM—and, in the process, shape China's destiny.

CHAPTER ONE

EARLY CHINESE CULTURE AND THE STRUGGLE FOR UNIFICATION

The earliest Chinese civilizations were established near the Yellow River, which cuts through the middle of modern-day China. In ancient times, being close to water meant controlling the agriculture that depended on it. These civilizations built their earliest structures from rammed earth, an early form of brickmaking that compressed a combination of soil and gravel to make floors and walls. Prehistoric Chinese people lived similarly to their neighbors in Central Asia: they grew millet and rice, raised domesticated animals, and used stone tools. They used cowrie shells as currency and made pottery without the use of a potter's wheel.

Prehistoric Chinese inventors, forgotten to time, drew on the natural world for inspiration. There are ancient archaeological remains of drinking vessels with traces of wine, suggesting that the Chinese discovered fermentation. China also invented sericulture: the use of silkworms to produce silk. Early sericulturists grew silkworms, which would build their cocoons in mulberry bushes. Craftswomen would then

boil the cocoons, untangle the fine silk threads, and weave shimmering fabric.

CHINESE DYNASTIES FORGE THEIR IDENTITY FROM MYTH AND BRONZE

According to traditional Chinese histories, the three first dynasties are the Xia (2100–1600 BCE), the Shang (1600–1050 BCE), and the Zhou (1046–256 BCE). Today, the Xia is understood as mythological—a fictional example made up by later scholars as a moral foundation for future dynasties. However, even the Xia myths contain important lessons about STEM in ancient China. Huangdi, the godlike "yellow emperor," was considered the father of agriculture and the inventor of China's first tools and weapons. Huangdi's wife, Leizu, was said to have invented silk weaving. Another legendary emperor, Yu the Great, was said to have tamed the waters of the flooding Yellow River by digging drainage canals.

The Shang dynasty is the first Chinese empire supported by objective historical evidence. This dynasty was a Bronze Age civilization, meaning that craftsmen learned to work with bronze to make tools, weapons, and ceremonial objects. At this time as well, people added wheat to their traditional diet of millet and rice. The standout feature of the Shang dynasty is the emperor's use of oracle bones to predict the future. These bones are the earliest source of Chinese writing in existence.

Around 1046 BCE, the Shang dynasty was overtaken by the Zhou dynasty. The Zhou created a

黄
帝

Huangdi, the mythical "yellow emperor" is said to have reigned from 2697 to 2597 BCE. Huangdi and his wife, Leizu, are considered the father and mother of China's oldest craft traditions.

more organized society; they governed from walled cities and established a land-distribution program called the well-field system. This system decreed that one-ninth of all private lands were the property of the Zhou, and the products of those lands would be reserved for taxes and redistribution. The Zhou expanded the making of bronze by conscripting forced laborers and experimented with early ironwork.

The Zhou dynasty was the first to fully commit to the Mandate of Heaven, which asserted that dynasties rose and fell based on their moral right to rule. To prove this, they turned to the sky for evidence. Believing themselves morally superior to the earlier Shang dynasty, the Zhou argued that signs from heaven demonstrated the legitimacy of their rule. Astrologers divided the sky into sections corresponding to different geographic regions. As the moon, stars, and occasional comets passed through the different regions, these movements were interpreted as omens for earthly events—similar to the interpretations of oracle bones. These early observations would pave the way for more systematic astronomy in the Han dynasty.

Despite Zhou confidence in their mandate, they faced many conflicts. Zhou armies fought against surrounding groups they believed to be uncivilized, especially the nomadic Xiongnu confederation. In addition, the Zhou struggled with internal instability, as multiple independent states broke off from the empire to compete for dominance. During the Zhou dynasty's conflicts, they devised one of the most powerful and influential weapons in ancient times: the crossbow. The crossbow fits a perpendicular stock to a traditional bow and fires using a mechanical trigger mechanism. This allows for greater speed, power, and accuracy. The very existence of these wood and bronze devices provides evidence of high social organization and technical skill.

Even with early STEM support, the Zhou would eventually lose their mandate, collapsing into several rival states that fought for influence. The next two periods—the Spring and Autumn period (771–453 BCE) and Warring States period (453–221 BCE)—together were the fire that sparked China's long history of STEM innovation. Though these periods were characterized by constant warfare, they also exhibited a war of ideas. As people competed to advance their political and religious views, many of them would shape how China saw itself and how China would approach science and technology in the coming generations.

SHANG ORACLE BONES AND THE ORIGIN OF CHINESE WRITING

Thousands of oracle bones have been discovered in ancient refuse heaps. They were used for predicting the future. The shoulder blades of cattle and the shells of tortoises would be placed in a fire, and the cracks in these bones would be interpreted to predict the outcomes of battles and harvests. Alongside symbols found on clay pots and bronze work from around the same time period, the writings on oracle bones are the earliest works that resemble the Chinese script as it is known today.

(continued on the next page)

(continued from the previous page)

Chinese writing is different from many other written languages because each character represents an entire word—not an individual letter. To master Chinese writing requires memorizing thousands of such characters. Chinese script influenced other languages of the region, including Japanese, Korean, and Vietnamese.

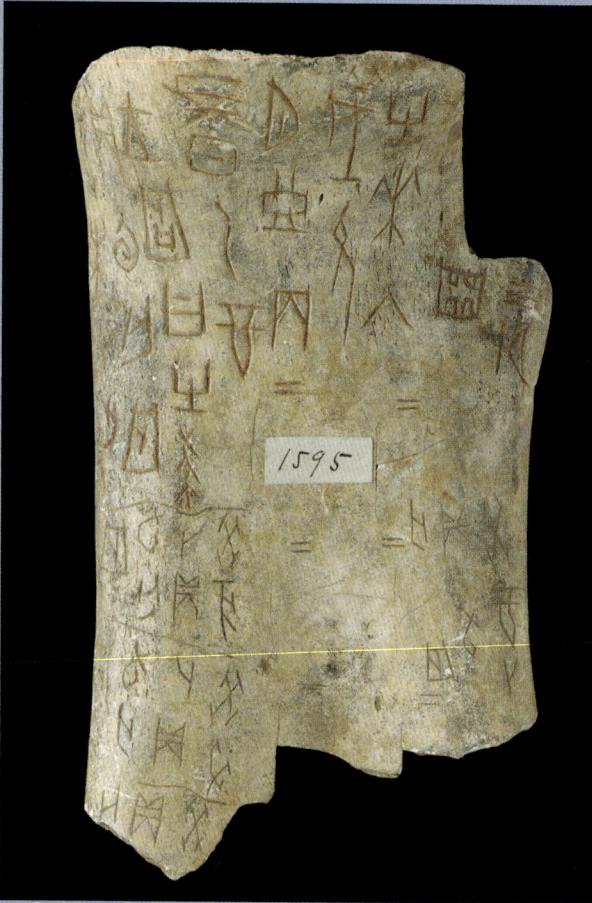

This oracle bone from the Shang dynasty includes predictions of the future: no ill omens will come in the next ten days. It also includes the modern Chinese character for "moon."

A DEBATE OVER STATE

In their early years, individual Chinese states had to manage large territories with competing factions among the elite. Ruling was a complex and unstable affair. In response, Chinese intellectuals spent a lot of time writing about how best to govern a country. The Spring and Autumn period is known for having the Hundred Schools of Thought emerge to try to solve the problem. For the philosophy of government, two of the most important ideas—Legalism and Confucianism—made the biggest impact.

Legalists believed that strict and severe laws, known as *fa*, were the best way to maintain order. Supporters of Legalism recommended that even minor rule breaking should be punished by torture and death. If a ruler's minister stepped outside of his official duties, he was to be executed. In an unstable time, Legalist-inspired rulers knew only one source of stability: strict, harsh law. The Legalists also paid attention to one scientific idea: that the success of a rule could be measured mathematically. As a result, they were very interested in population figures and standardized measurements.

The teachings of the Legalists would end up going only so far in securing future Chinese states. A competing view would shape Chinese history: the writings of Confucius (551–479 BCE). Confucius advocated for *li*, or proper conduct in government, religious, and family affairs. Confucius argued that each person should turn to ancient rituals and

至聖孔子

名丘字仲尼山東
兗州府曲阜縣人

Confucius was and is considered China's most important philosopher. His ethical teachings left their mark on the Chinese government and became the model for all aspiring bureaucrats.

traditions as a guide for virtuous behavior. If everyone was respectful to his or her superiors and generous to his or her subordinates, Confucius believed that China would be peaceful and prosperous. Confucius collected the most important writings from ancient China, especially in history and literature. The writings of Confucius and his followers—plus the older classics he compiled—became a standard part of Chinese education up to the beginning of the twentieth century.

During the Hundred Schools period, the earliest Chinese scientific traditions emerged as well. They came from an unexpected source: religion and divination. The doctrine of the Mandate of Heaven directed rulers' attention to the stars, and this search for omens helped develop disciplines like astronomy. One unusual divination practice was conducted by throwing reed sticks and interpreting the patterns they made when they fell. The *I-Ching*—a book that added logical rules for interpretation—was the culmination of that process. Many practitioners of the *I-Ching* went on to create other tools for prediction, which would result in the invention of the compass centuries later.

The religion of Taoism, which rejected society to explore the inner workings of nature, made a special contribution to STEM in China. Founded by the philosopher and writer Lao Tzu, Taoism taught the principle of wu wei, or "acting in accordance with nature." This rule was both a personal ideal and a motivation to solve problems by working to understand them. Taoists devised three important concepts that they used to understand the natural world. The first was yin-yang, which explained opposing principles, such as light and dark, dry and wet, hot and cold, and others, as being in continual balance. Originally applying these concepts to the cycle of the seasons, Taoists began to apply the concept to other cycles: the stars, human history, and living beings. To make these analogies more precise and useful, the Taoists developed a second concept, the idea of the "five phases," which could be compared to ancient Greek beliefs that all things were made up of four elements. The Chinese believed that the elements of wood, fire, earth, metal, and water corresponded to five phases of transformation. Lastly, qi was a spiritual energy that took various forms in matter.

Some of the earliest applications for Taoist principles were in medicine. Taoists studied the relationship between the circulation of the blood and the cycle of breathing, believing that the two were distinct qi in a harmonious yin-yang relationship. Ancient Chinese doctors developed the practice of acupuncture, in which tiny needles were inserted at key circulation points determined by this system. In later dynasties, many of China's great inventors drew on other Taoist and *I-Ching* principles to conduct experiments, resulting in inventions that would change the world.

CHAPTER TWO

QIN AND HAN CENTRALIZATION AND GLORY

I n 221 BCE, the chaos of the Warring States period was brought to a close, and the Qin dynasty unified all of China. The Qin and Han dynasties are understood as the beginning of Imperial China. These dynasties dominated the region, centralizing the economy, launching public works projects, and developing the fundamental sciences that would later shape Chinese industry.

THE QIN AND HAN ENGINEERING MARVELS

From a modern perspective, the Qin dynasty's reputation is poor. Qin leaders adopted principles of Legalism, permitting extreme punishment for lawbreakers. In addition, the Qin dynasty was opposed to book learning. Chinese sources describe Qin authorities burning books and executing scholars. Though some of these accounts were likely exaggerated, the state largely did not concern itself with scholarly pursuits. However, the orderly Qin regime introduced one important scientific feature to Chinese life: standardization. Under the Qin, standard

秦始皇

Qin Shi Huangdi was the first ruler of the Qin dynasty. Unlike prior "kings," Qin Shi Huangdi styled himself "emperor" to envision a single unified Chinese empire. Like his successors, he was invested in advancing STEM.

weights and lengths were put into place, and even tools like ox-cart gauges were ordered to follow identical patterns. Currency was reformed, and the written language was regulated so that everyone in the empire could understand it more easily.

The Qin dynasty is also distinguished by its massive construction projects. Workers were gathered by the hundreds of thousands and forced to build roads, walls, buildings, and waterworks. A grand imperial highway system was built that included more roads than even the Roman Empire did at its peak. To transport grain throughout the empire, a canal was built to link the Yangtze and West Rivers. Qin emperors also commenced the construction of what would later become the Great Wall of China.

Despite some STEM innovation, the Qin dynasty did not last longer than a generation. In 206 BCE, the Han dynasty took control, building an empire that rivaled the Roman Empire in size and power. The Han dynasty rejected Legalism in favor of Confucianism, requiring that all bureaucrats learn the teachings of the revered philosopher. The Han centralized the economy by setting up state monopolies on the production of salt and iron. Silk production became a major industry. Han silks traveled as far as Rome, over informal trade routes that would eventually become known as the Silk Road.

In ancient China, salt and iron production were big businesses. Salt was an essential component of people's diet, and iron was used to make cutting-edge tools and weapons. In the late second century CE, Han emperor Wudi took control of these industries

A bronze stirrup from the sixth or seventh century CE is shown here. This simple invention revolutionized warfare and would become a common feature of both Chinese cavalry and the nomadic tribes they warred against.

as a way to finance the military. Eventually, iron and salt were responsible for half of state tax revenues. Although Confucian traditionalists protested what they saw as the dishonor of state-run commerce, they lost the debate. This laid the foundation for a pattern of state-controlled trade and industry that ran through the rest of Chinese history.

Along with these dramatic political turns, Han dynasty advances in iron casting led to a large variety of widespread household tools. The stirrup, a metal footrest attached to riding saddles, made horseback riding dramatically easier. The moldboard plow, which would spark an agricultural revolution in Europe almost two millennia later, opened up available farmland in China. Iron cooking pots were commonplace. All of these tools could be found across the country due to technological advances and state controls on the iron industry.

One everyday invention, especially, changed the world: the wheelbarrow. Chinese historians describe how, during the first century BCE, Taoist scholar Ko Yu invented a "wooden goat," which could wheel hundreds of pounds up and down the countryside. Wheelbarrows of different sizes and shapes were designed according to terrain and purpose. Some even had sails, allowing rapid wind-powered transport across the countryside. The wheelbarrow was so important for military supply chains that the specifications of its construction were kept secret for centuries.

GREAT WALL, LONG PROCESS

The Great Wall of China is one of the most magnificent human-made structures in history. Stretching across 13,000 miles (21,000 kilometers), the wall as it stands today is primarily constructed from bricks, with fortified watchtowers. The process of its creation took thousands of years and the lives of millions of laborers to complete.

During the Qin and Han dynasties, the major external threat to China was the Huns—a nomadic people from

The stone construction and evenly spaced guard towers in this section of the Great Wall in modern-day Hebei Province date this portion to the Ming dynasty.

the steppes. Prior states had built defensive walls, which the Qin unified and lengthened. The Han dynasty would pick up the job, continuing the construction of the wall over hundreds of years. At first, the "Long Wall," as it was called, was built primarily of rammed earth to limit the amount of transportation needed to bring supplies to the construction site.

Maintaining and rebuilding the wall became a priority for many dynasties, especially the later Ming dynasty (1368–1644 CE). Ming leaders were especially keen to protect themselves from nomadic invaders and continued expanding the wall throughout the dynasty. They clad the rammed earth structures with the bricks that make up the wall today. Construction stopped only in 1644 when invaders marched through the gates, took power, and founded the Qing dynasty.

HAN ASTRONOMY AND ITS EARTHLY IMPACTS

The main STEM achievements of the Han dynasty stemmed from official support for astronomy. Research into the heavens helped support a range of developments, including mechanical engineering, geography, and mathematics.

When a new dynasty was declared, it was customary to redesign the calendar. These calendars drew on astronomical signs as evidence of the dynasty's Mandate of Heaven and also helped coordinate the timing of growing seasons with religious rites. As a result, court astronomers were important figures who observed the heavens closely to aid their mathematical calculations of more earthly matters. Astronomers were mathematicians, geographers, and engineers, all rolled into one.

Chinese astronomers believed that the sun and stars rotated around the Earth. Although this idea was eventually proven false, it led to a remarkable creation: the armillary sphere. The armillary sphere was a mechanical device that represented the relative movements of the stars and planets through the year. These finely crafted devices were the precursors of mechanical clocks. China also developed many mathematical traditions to support state efforts. They devised mathematical solutions to important problems in construction and the distribution of resources.

Along with the famous abacus—an early calculation tool that represented numbers with beads and rods—Han China also developed counting rods as a written means of representing numbers. Han mathematicians experimented with negative numbers and developed a positional notation with an empty mark: for example, the 0 in 105. This notation was the first step toward the revolutionary concept of zero, invented in India centuries later.

ZHANG HENG, CHINA'S "STAR" INVENTOR

Zhang Heng (78–139 CE) was one of China's greatest inventors. He was an official astrologer for the Han dynasty, and, in this role, he devised innovative theories of the heavens. He revolutionized mapmaking with the use of grid layouts and scaled distances. These standards allowed a more accurate survey of distances, helping soldiers, officials, and merchants travel the countryside.

However, his most celebrated invention is the seismograph. Unlike modern-day devices, which electronically measure the vibrations of the earth, Zhang Heng's seismograph was an elaborate mechanism of decorated bronze. In Zhang Heng's device, a pendulum at the center was surrounded by eight carved dragons, each with a ball in its mouth and a carved frog underneath. The earthquake would slightly shift the casing and cause just one ball to fall into the frog's open mouth—from the dragon facing in the direction of the earthquake. Chinese histories record that Zhang Heng's device was able to record an earthquake taking place in a town several days' travel away. Modern researchers have reconstructed the device, which acts according to traditional descriptions.

Zhang Heng provided the Han with many innovations in astronomy, geography, and engineering. Because the

(continued on the next page)

25

(continued from the previous page)

Shown here is a reconstructed model of Zhang Heng's seismograph. Each carefully placed frog waits with an open mouth to receive a ball released by a distant earthquake.

Han dynasty took seriously the importance of scientific research, scientists learned not only about abstract principles, but also about applied techniques that shaped the Chinese empire.

THE FIRST GREAT INVENTION: PAPER

Since the development of writing, ancient civilizations struggled with finding a convenient medium for carrying it. As empires grew, they needed a cheap, reliable form of conveying the thousands of reports related to the daily routines of ruling. For a time, important Chinese texts were written on slips of bamboo and fine silk. The problem with silk was that it was too expensive; the problem with bamboo was that it was too heavy. Emperor Qin Shi Huang (259–210 BCE) of the Qin dynasty complained that the volume of reports and laws was too cumbersome. These bamboo slips were so bulky that the emperor was reading hundreds of pounds of letters every day.

Unlike other writing media, the production of paper involves more chemical knowledge. In China, materials such as bark and cloth rags were pulverized and boiled, then pounded flat and dried until the material formed a flat surface. The first paper is attributed to Han-era inventor Cai Lun and was perfected over the Tang dynasty. At first, paper was made from refuse cloth, and its function as a disposable writing medium was not yet defined. People even used this early paper as a form of clothing. Military technicians invented hard paper armor, reportedly as sturdy as metal.

However, once people started incorporating mulberry bark in papermaking, paper started to look like modern paper. The Tang dynasty began designating special districts, such as Sichuan, as official paper factories. Papermaking became an art form in its own right. No longer coarse and rough, special artisans developed techniques for paper of different colors, with stamps and decorations, all of which became components of the literary culture that the Tang dynasty would later cultivate.

CHAPTER THREE

SUI AND TANG PUBLIC WORKS AND COMMERCE

After the collapse of the Han dynasty in 220 CE, China experienced another period of fragmentation and competing states that would last for centuries. Farmers grew for subsistence only, the use of money declined, and innovation was low. Emperor Wendi of the Sui dynasty (581–618 CE) finally reunified China. Sui reforms and innovations were continued by the Tang dynasty (618–907 CE). Massive public works were begun, religious life transformed, and the government established a core tradition: the imperial civil service exam. Tang rule in China catalyzed another golden age, distinguished by commerce, fine arts, and the expansion of cities.

SOCIAL TRANSFORMATION IN THE SUI AND TANG DYNASTIES

Tang China experienced rapid urbanization. Chang'an—the capital during both the Sui and Tang dynasties—became the largest city in the world. Chang'an at its peak had one million inhabitants, including a large number of visiting foreign traders. As the center for the imperial exam, scholars from around the country enriched Chang'an's intellectual life, all hoping to join the privileged bureaucratic class, after proving they were well versed in the scholarly history of Confucius.

Chang'an and other cities were extensively planned. The imperial palace of Chang'an occupied the north-central section of the city, reflecting the emperor's central importance to the kingdom. The city was built around the palace according to a rectangular grid system, with streets sectioning off smaller neighborhoods and the two main markets. These areas were more tightly regulated than most modern cities. Individual neighborhoods had nightly curfews, and the two markets were the only places where large-scale commerce was allowed.

Chinese dynasties had been historically hostile to open trade, but the Sui and Tang dynasties loosened these restrictions. Urban planning brought craftspeople together to increase production of goods, and canals allowed the transportation of

These coins—minted during the Tang dynasty—display a central hole, characteristic of Chinese coins, which allowed merchants to keep their money together with a thread.

goods across the empire. Copper money was also introduced during this time.

Chinese society was transformed by Buddhism, a religion named after the Buddha, an Indian sage from the time of Confucius. The Buddha taught detachment from earthly possessions to achieve spiritual bliss and escape the cycle of rebirth. This foreign faith appealed to impoverished people especially, spreading from India across Asia via the Silk Road. In earlier dynasties, Buddhism was suppressed and treated with suspicion. By the Tang dynasty, a form of Buddhism called Chan Buddhism—known in the West as Zen—became an official religion. These religious changes were instrumental to another of the great inventions: the printing press.

THE GRAND CANAL: A "GREAT WALL" OF RIVER TRANSPORT

Advances in hydraulic engineering, which was used to build canals, dams, and reservoirs, are less flashy than those that led to the Great Wall or an armillary sphere. However, hydraulic engineering is extremely important in both the STEM history and cultural legends of the Chinese dynasties. The Sui Grand Canal is like a Great

Wall: massive in scope and of monumental importance in Chinese history.

The Grand Canal linked several canals in a continuous waterway from Luoyang to the Yangtze River—equivalent to half the length of the United States' Eastern Seaboard. At its highest points, the canal's terrain was more than 100 feet (30 meters) above sea level, requiring the innovative use of lock gates. This invention closed a section of a canal, then raised or lowered the water level to allow a ship to pass. The same underlying principle is used in canals in modern times.

This Qing dynasty map of the Grand Canal was made well after the canal system's construction, but many of the lock gates in the illustration were devised in the earliest stages of the project.

PRINTING EXPANDS RELIGIOUS AND CULTURAL LITERACY

Paper had been invented during the Han dynasty, and by the Tang dynasty, papermaking had become a refined art form. The process of making bark paper and bamboo paper had been perfected, and artisans were using dyes and gold dust to make paper beautiful to look at and hold. However, this art would soon be overtaken by an even more important invention: printing.

Before their mass production, books were copied by hand. This was not only a time-consuming and expensive process, but it also increased the risk of inaccuracies in reproducing the book. For example, copies of Marco Polo's book describing his voyages in China were hand copied, and each is different from the next. This is because the people employed to copy these books were prone to mistakes. In the case of special texts—such as the writings of Confucius or the teachings of Buddhism—there was a major incentive to create a more precise and simple way of reproducing books. This would not only guarantee the purity of the texts themselves, but also help spread important religious, intellectual, and cultural thought more effectively.

The primary mode of printing that emerged in China was block printing, in which an entire page was carved into a flat block of wood, covered with ink, and then stamped onto paper. Wood was chosen for medium hardness and high absorbency, commonly that from fruit trees. A calligrapher would write an original copy on thin, waxed paper, then a carver would engrave through the paper backwards, so it would print the right way. A printer could then use this block to print more than a thousand pages per day.

Along with the appeal of Buddhism, printing was driven by the needs of the Chinese government. With such extensive historical records and a long tradition of scholarship on matters of state, there was a drive to print important texts for bureaucrats across the country. As a result, China enjoyed a print culture in which books were cheaper than anywhere else in the world. Even after the invention of the European printing press, visitors to China were stunned by the broad availability of printed material. These books gave more people access to the required education to participate in government service.

During the Song dynasty (960–1279 CE), China would beat Europe to another printing milestone: movable type printing. Movable type casts molds of individual characters, allowing the molds to be reassembled for each book. Chinese type molds were made of tin, clay, or wax. However, movable type was not as popular in China as it would become in Europe. Due to the thousands of characters in the Chinese language, producing type molds was cumbersome and expensive. Block printing would remain the dominant medium for spreading the written word for centuries to come.

CHINESE ADVANCES THAT CONQUERED TIME AND SPACE

In early Chinese society, a deep concern with omens had led scholars and leaders to look carefully at the stars; these observations then translated into mechanical inventions like the armillary sphere. During the Sui and Tang dynasties, this pattern continued, yielding not one but two revolutionary inventions: the mechanical clock and the compass. The mechanical clock changed human understanding of time; the compass provided an improved mastery of space.

The mechanical clock was originally an adaptation of the armillary sphere. Chinese emperors wanted to determine the precise timings of important events so their astrologers could interpret the astrological significance of when they took place. To create a machine that could rotate in sync with the turning of a day was an enormous design challenge. The difficulty was figuring out how to mechanically transfer continuous movement into regular repeating events. Yi Xing, an astronomer and inventor, successfully produced such a device in 725 CE. It used a consistent water source to fill successions of troughs attached to a wheel. Once a trough filled, the counterweight would cause the trough to jerk away. Later engineers would replace the water with a pendulum fixed to a grooved escapement gear, a mechanism still used in pocket watches today.

The development of the compass was based on a similar combination of magical beliefs and genuine science. Taoists had long been interested in magnets, analyzing their special qi and experimenting with the magnetic properties of iron as it was heated and cooled. Practitioners of the *I-Ching* spun magnetized spoons on a special divining board, and the precursor to the compass was born. These divining boards were most frequently used for feng shui, a religious practice that placed great importance on the proper arrangement of buildings and their interiors.

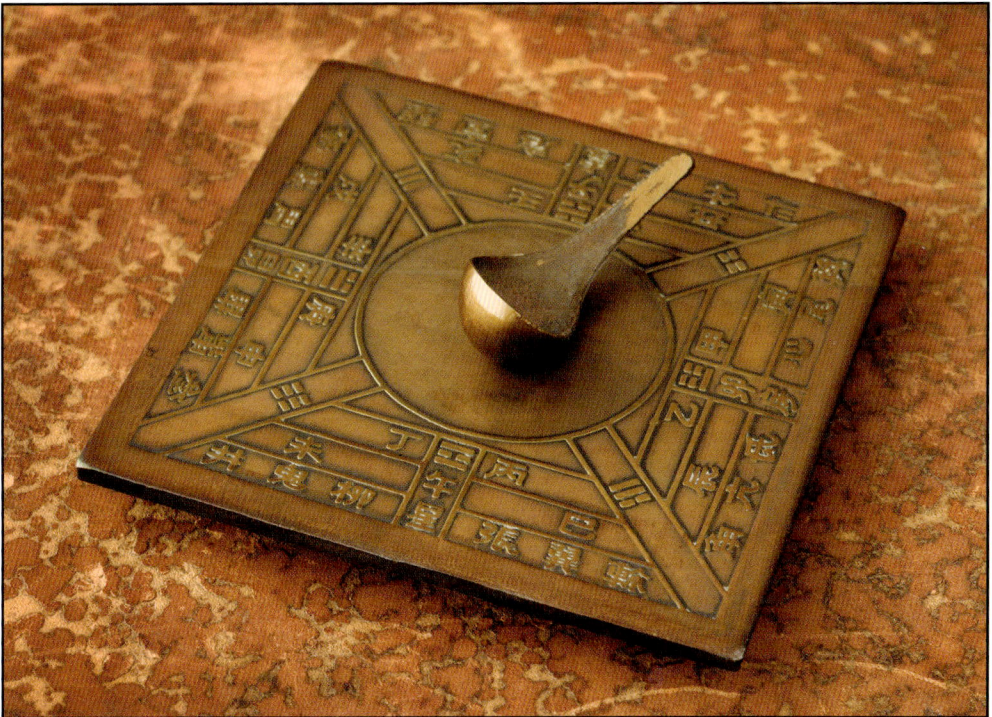

The symbolic carvings on this reproduction of a Han-era spoon and divining board—an ancestor to the compass—attest to the compass's mystical origins.

By the Tang dynasty, it was common practice for Taoist priests to use divining boards with a floating magnetized needle, known as a wet compass. In addition to their religious uses, they were utilized as a mathematical tool for calculating direction. The dry compass, which used steel needles in a spinning mechanical frame, began to appear between the Tang and Song dynasties. This invention would also spread to the Arab and European world, launching a new age for sea trade. Even in the twenty-first century, compasses are still a crucial component of navigation, particularly in sea and air travel.

CHAPTER FOUR

THE SONG DYNASTY GOES TO SEA

During the Tang dynasty, China's changing economy led to an urbanized society, with a much greater role for manufacturing and trade. When the Tang dynasty collapsed and Emperor Taizu proclaimed the Song dynasty in 960, China became a major sea power and its economy evolved and unified, selling manufactured trade goods in enormous ships. These changes led to a rise of culture, prosperity, and regional prestige. In addition, Taoist alchemy yielded China's most explosive invention: gunpowder. This last STEM innovation helped the Song dynasty during the many wars they fought in this time.

THE SONG'S INDUSTRIAL REVOLUTION

Song China became a fully linked national economy, which allowed the Central Kingdom to dramatically scale up the manufacturing of goods. The first development was agricultural: the introduction of fast-growing, drought-resistant champa rice. Originally appearing in Vietnam, Chinese officials introduced this breed to the rice-growing southern part of the country. In the north, where agriculture was more vulnerable to floods and droughts,

millions of tons of rice were shipped annually up the Grand Canal, which helped stabilize population growth. The result of these agricultural changes was regional economic specialization, with the north focusing on manufacturing and the south focusing on agriculture.

Improvements in silk making, ceramics, metalwork, and shipping allowed for the production of goods to improve, scale more efficiently, and be distributed to consumers. Objects once considered luxuries—porcelains, silverware, combs, lacquerware, and silks—were mass-produced, varied in style and fashion, and sold widely. The invention of the treadle silk frame, which used a foot pump to spin thread, led to the expansion of silk weaving across the countryside. Richer fabrics were produced in greater numbers than were seen before or after, until the introduction of industrial silk making in the nineteenth century.

In the Song capital of Kaifeng, advances in metallurgy and machines were applied to the massive production of military weapons. STEM advancement in metal forging led workers to start using coal as fuel, which provided the consistent high temperatures needed for elaborate iron casting. Geared waterwheels used river power to automate metal hammering and temperature-controlling air pumps. The state employed thousands of artisans in dedicated divisions: hand weapons, armor, siege weapons, dried goods, and even gas refining. These artisans produced millions of crossbows and hand weapons each year and thousands of suits of armor. Kaifeng was a national industrial powerhouse.

This nineteenth-century engraving by Thomas Allom introduced European audiences to Chinese technology. The waterwheel depicted is an example of Chinese inventors' ability to harness water power for a variety of purposes.

Even with all the metallurgical and agricultural advancements during the Song dynasty, the product that defined the era was ceramics. Porcelain, the highest-grade ceramic requiring high temperatures to fire, was expanded with the use of coal fuel. Potters developed the dragon kiln, which connected several kilns in a row up a hill, to allow hot air to rise up the kiln and fire more ceramics at once. These dragon kilns were early iterations of ceramics factories, firing thousands of vessels at once. As a result, porcelain and stoneware became commonly used across China. Indeed, one luxury porcelain became so popular that

Shown here is a funerary jar featuring an elaborate dragon figure baked into the design. The green celadon glaze was a hallmark of Song dynasty ceramics and made it a high-value status object.

Song royalty adopted another style to ensure that the court was always ahead of the fashion.

Chinese ceramics became the country's signature trade good, shipped across the Indian Ocean and reaching as far as Cairo. This popularity has led some historians to call China's sea shipping routes the Ceramics Road, because, like the Silk Road, it formed a first pillar of Chinese global trade. Many archaeological sites in Asia and the Persian Gulf have revealed Chinese ceramics with Arabic decorations, suggesting that Chinese artisans were manufacturing goods designed specifically to be sold in foreign markets.

PAPER MONEY TAKES FLIGHT IN A NATIONAL ECONOMY

By the Song dynasty, paper money was an official currency whose production was controlled by the government. This currency, termed "flying money," was preceded by private bills of credit, transferred between merchants. Independent financial institutions began producing these bills, which began to be used as money. In 1023 CE, the government assumed complete control of the production of paper money.

As in modern times, currency printers devised techniques to ensure that the bills could not be

(continued on the next page)

(continued from the previous page)

counterfeited, such as printing in multiple layers of colors to make the bills difficult to copy. Though paper money facilitated trade, it came with the risk of currency inflation. During times of economic trouble, the bills could quickly lose their value. Still, the invention would transform the world economy, as Marco Polo would help introduce the idea to Europe centuries later.

CHINA BUILDS SHIPS AT UNFATHOMABLE SCALES

During the medieval period, the Indian Ocean was the center of world trade as the meeting point of Africa, the Persian Gulf, the Indian subcontinent, and Asia. Europe, mostly cut off from the world after the collapse of the Roman Empire, was geographically isolated during this prolific period of trading. Sailors followed a schedule set by the monsoon winds, which changed direction from east to west twice a year.

Arab and Persian merchants initially dominated trade in the Indian Ocean. By the Song dynasty, though, China had taken over this market both by the volume of its trade and the quality of its ships. Part of this shift was due to the use of the mariner's compass, which revolutionized navigation. China also began to transform ship design. While Arab vessels were simple and small, Chinese vessels eventually became much bigger. These innovations were helped by the overall expansion of trade during the Tang dynasty. With a stronger economy—which made trade goods easier to manufacture—there was enough capital to invest in developing new ships.

China had developed many of its shipping innovations for use in river transport, including the distinctive junk design and sternpost rudder for navigation. As these junks were outfitted for sea voyages, several important innovations became standard. For example, ships were divided into bulkheads, or watertight sections that allowed the ship to remain afloat in case of a flooded compartment. Chinese ships also used multiple masts to allow the sails to harness additional wind power. Combat ships were outfitted with armor plating and gunpowder weapons. All of these STEM innovations—born in China—would be adopted by rival powers in the ensuing centuries.

These ships were some of the largest wooden vessels ever built. At over 100 feet (30 m) in length and with crews of hundreds of people, Chinese ships dwarfed the competition. By comparison, the ships used in Columbus's voyages to North America were half the size of most Chinese deep-sea vessels. Later, during the Ming dynasty, the government would build fleets of 200-foot (60 m) "treasure ships," laden with riches, on diplomatic voyages across the Indian Ocean.

FROM TAOIST ELIXIRS TO EXPLOSIVE "FIRE MEDICINE"

The origins of gunpowder begin with the alchemical research of the Taoists during the Tang dynasty. Like Europeans in the same period, Taoist alchemists combined substances with the dream of turning lead into gold and creating immortality potions. Despite these far-fetched goals, the work itself was genuine science. Taoist monks built household laboratories, took detailed notes, and repeated experiments. They used the terms of the time to explain chemical properties according to yin-yang and the five phases. When these early researchers combined charcoal, sulfur, and saltpeter (potassium nitrate), the results were explosive—and gunpowder, or "fire medicine," was born.

Early researchers tried different ratios of ingredients to determine how fire medicine worked, discovering that tilting the balance toward nitrates or toward sulfur led to different varieties of explosions. These results were eventually tailored to a range of weapons and even recreational devices. Along with the guns and cannons used to conquer the world, gunpowder improved civil engineering and led to the principles that are still used in modern rocket and engine design.

China developed an enormous array of gunpowder weapons: cattle-shaped "fire oxen" that spit gunpowder-fueled fire, "thunderclap bombs," "great leather bombs," the imaginatively named

五重裹衣以麻縛定更別鎔松脂傅之以砲故復有

清油桐油濃油同熬成膏入前藥末旋和勻以紙

研乾漆搗為末竹茹麻茹即微炒為碎末黃蠟松脂

右以晉州硫黃窩黃焰硝同搗羅砒黃定粉黃丹同

桐油半兩松脂十四兩濃油一分

竹茹一兩黃丹一兩黃蠟半兩清油一分

麻茹一兩乾漆一兩砒黃一兩定粉一兩

晉州硫黃十四兩窩黃七兩焰硝二斤半

火藥法

右隨砲預備用以蓋覆及防火箭

鐵三具 氈一領 鑡三具 火索一十條

唧筒四箇 土布袋二十五條 界欐索一十條

水濊二箇 拒馬二 麻搭四具 小水桶二隻

鐵鈎十八箇 大末樵二箇 界扎索一十條

散子末二百五十條 救火大桶二

拐頭柱一十八條 皮簾八片 皮索一十條

鐵火

This Song-era recipe for gunpowder is taken from the *Wujing Zongyao*, an influential compendium of Chinese military science. Along with gunpowder, the text also includes designs for devices like catapults and warships.

"heaven-shaking thunder bomb," and arsenic-filled poison smoke bombs. The most common weapon was the fire lance, a gunpowder-filled bamboo tube that served as a five-minute disposable flamethrower. These, plus catapult-launched iron bombs, were indispensable for the Song's many military conflicts.

Eventually, the enormous range of colorfully named weapons became the weapons adopted by the rest of the world—especially Europe. Bombs became increasingly reliable in warfare by 1200 CE. Fire lances eventually evolved into muskets and rockets by the end of the thirteenth century. Chinese technicians were especially adept at designing rockets, inventing the two-stage rockets that exploded at long distances, as well as wheelbarrow-mounted rocket frames that could shoot dozens of rockets at once.

In addition to these powerful military applications, gunpowder would change the world in other ways. Gunpowder was used extensively in mining and civil engineering, making resources more available and aiding in massive construction projects. More importantly, the energy released by gunpowder revealed the principles of internal combustion in other fuels. Without knowing its Chinese origin, European inventors drew on the mechanical principles of the cannon to devise the working parts of the steam engine. Though Chinese and European experiments with gunpowder engines both failed, the cars, trains, and rockets of the present day all owe a debt to Chinese fire medicine.

CHAPTER FIVE

A MONGOL DYNASTY: CONQUEST AND CONTACT

Throughout China's history, each dynasty had an uneasy relationship with the nomadic ethnic groups neighboring them. This tension often took the form of invasions from the nomads, periodic attempts in return to conquer more territory for China, and a strong interest in militarized defensive walls. Though the Song dynasty was one of the peaks of China's power, it was ultimately conquered by history's most powerful group of nomads: the Mongol Empire.

THE NOMADS STRIKE BACK

By the thirteenth century, China had established its dominance over Indian Ocean trade, with manufacturing power amazingly resembling the present day. Despite the use of gunpowder in warfare, the Chinese military was weak in one fundamental area: the cavalry. Horses and other domesticated animals are an overlooked part of the history of technology; animals are the first engines, and in medieval warfare, horses were indispensable. Due to the Song dynasty's ongoing conflicts with surrounding nomads, who controlled access to the strongest horse

breeds, China was unable to defend itself against the world's most successful cavalry force.

A Mongol warrior named Temujin—after more than a decade of warfare with other nomadic tribes—achieved the impossible and united them all, proclaiming himself Genghis Khan: "universal ruler." Believing himself destined to conquer the world, he led an enormous, disciplined, and brutal army to build the largest land empire in human history, spanning from China to eastern Europe. Early on, Mongol warfare relied on one seemingly simple piece of technology: the stirrup. As early as the third century CE, the stirrup was in use by Chinese cavalry, its primary function to stabilize a standing rider. This Chinese invention allowed a soldier to fight and shoot arrows while maintaining mobility—an enormous battlefield advantage. As it would happen, the Mongol Empire began with the use of this invention.

Mongol armies devised a wood-reinforced saddle that, when combined with stirrups, allowed a soldier to ride while standing securely, freely twisting and turning to launch arrows accurately while the horse maneuvered. The genius of this innovation was not in coming up with an elaborate, specialized technology, but in adopting the tactics best suited to the technology that was already available. Using this saddle-and-stirrup combination, Mongol cavalry was a maneuverable attack force that could rapidly fire arrows in any direction, in addition to fielding faster, taller soldiers on horseback. No contemporaneous land army could stand a chance.

This portrait of Genghis Khan appears in an album of Yuan emperors. The illustration style, similar to other imperial portraits, reflects the Mongol adoption of many Chinese traditions.

After the Mongols conquered the surrounding nomadic tribes, they faced a new challenge: getting past the walled cities of settled populations. The major cities in China and Eurasia employed walled defenses and had practice with holding off sieges. Song China had held off countless invading armies on the strength of their fire lances, using their gunpowder fuel as an almost magical advantage to scorch would-be conquerors. Unfortunately for the Chinese, as Mongols chipped away at their defenses, the invaders found a solution: drafting captured Chinese technicians into the army. Along with exploiting the new gunpowder technology, Mongols adopted other Chinese siege engines, such as battering rams, scaling ladders, and catapults.

As the Mongol Empire began to conquer eastern Europe and parts of the Middle East, Chinese technicians went with them. Many of the conscripted technicians became high-ranking soldiers in their own right. Without them, the Mongol conquest of the Arab world would have been much more difficult. Though Genghis Khan died in 1227, his sons and grandsons continued the conquest until 16 percent of the world was under Mongol control. The empire was divided into four regional khanates, separate divisions ruled by a different descendant of Genghis Khan. One of them, Kublai Khan, proclaimed himself emperor of a new Chinese dynasty: the Yuan. After thousands of years of Chinese conflicts with nomadic tribes, one such tribe had finally won the Mandate of Heaven.

MONGOL RULE AND CULTURAL TRANSMISSIONS

After the enormous casualties of the Mongol campaigns—during which millions of people were killed—the Mongol Empire was comparatively tolerant. They frequently supported the religions and cultures of the people they conquered, often adopting those groups' own cultural practices. For example, the Uighur writing system became the standard writing system of the Mongol language. Yuan dynasty China, especially under Kublai Khan, offered patronage to Confucianism and the arts.

Most importantly, the Mongol Empire's aggressive expansion allowed for enormous amounts of cultural exchange. The wars themselves led to encounters between Arabs, Indians, Chinese, Persians, and Europeans, leading to ideas moving back and forth between these formerly isolated peoples. Arab algebra spread east and west, while many signature Chinese inventions (especially gunpowder) began the process of diffusion westward. The Silk Road was secured under what is now known as the Pax Mongolica, and trade was accelerated.

These secure lines of communication led to the most consequential cross-cultural contact in the world:

(continued on the next page)

(continued from the previous page)

the travels of Marco Polo. The young Italian merchant traveled with his father and uncle across the Silk Road to China, where he became an adviser to Kublai Khan. When Polo returned home, his reports of China's fabulous wealth, culture, and technology were an inspiration for Europeans to explore—and explore they did. Adopting Chinese STEM advancements, Christopher Columbus attempted to find a sea route to Polo's fabled China. He arrived in the Americas instead, beginning a new era of discovery, violence, and exchange.

A European depiction of Marco Polo's journey to China and back, this illustration's heavily stylized features suggest that Europe had not yet caught up to Chinese advances in cartography.

YUAN ADVANCES IN MATHEMATICS, ASTRONOMY, AND GEOGRAPHY

Mongol cultural exchanges led to advances in geography and the paired disciplines of astronomy and mathematics. Having united so many disparate places and peoples, the discipline of geography experienced massive advances, best exemplified by the work of Zhu Siben. This mapmaker built on the grid-array invented by Han genius Zhang Heng, which he used to create the most precise and complete map of the known world. Between 1311 and 1320 CE, Zhu Siben collected geographic data from taxation reports, using this information to assemble a huge map of Europe, Africa, and Asia. He corrected inaccurate European representations of Africa, as European mapmakers had mistakenly assumed Africa's southern coast pointed east. The importance of maps in the ancient world cannot be overstated; for anyone—ruler, peasant, merchant, or explorer—knowing where to go and how to get there was a major part of life. Accurate maps were worth their weight in gold for navigators and intellectuals who wanted to better understand the world. Zhu Siben's work influenced world cartography for centuries after his death.

In addition to advances in geography, Yuan China would also benefit from innovations in astronomy and mathematics. Kublai Khan's court astronomer, Guo Shoujing, was a polymath, like Zhang Heng. Guo built armillary spheres, pursued hydraulic engineering, and devised mathematical formulas for calculating the movements of the sun. His work was expansive; not only did his calculations echo the later techniques of trigonometry, but his equatorial system for mapping the stars eventually became the standard model of astronomy worldwide.

Shown here is a portrait of Kublai Khan, grandson of Genghis Khan and founder of the Yuan dynasty. Unlike his more violent grandfather, Kublai was relatively moderate in his rule.

After Chinese encounters with Arabic algebra, Yuan mathematicians began solving new problems. Zhu Shijie—another innovative mathematician—devised solutions for multivariable simultaneous equations, polynomials of any degree, and sums of infinite series. Zhu Shijie's math closely resembled later European innovations, such as matrix notation and Pascal's triangle, but Chinese influence on these formulations was minimal. Chinese mathematics, unfortunately, did not spread as widely as compasses and firearm technology. Mathematical solutions, even far-reaching ones like Zhu Shijie's and Guo Shoujing's, were devised to solve engineering problems and were never standardized as a general theory. Chinese mathematics was innovative, but not highly influential at a global level.

Though the Mongol Empire was an obvious disruption of China's pristine self-identity, the repercussions were extremely consequential for world history. Through the combination of violent conquest and tolerant rule, the Mongols inadvertently caused a great mixing of ideas that changed the balance of power. Europe, now fully exposed to Chinese (and Arabic) scientific innovations, would begin to dominate world affairs. Though China would eventually overthrow the ruling Yuan dynasty, the succeeding Ming and Qing dynasties would increasingly exist under a European shadow.

CHAPTER SIX

MING AND CHING DYNASTIES LOSE FOOTING IN THE NEW WORLD ECONOMY

The last two Chinese dynasties were the Ming (1368–1644 CE) and the Qing (1644–1912 CE). Both dynasties relied on the substantial revenues from their trade goods, which China sold to Europe in exchange for silver. Under the Ming dynasty, Chinese STEM reached its ultimate peaks. Many important developments in naval technology, traditional medicine, and civil engineering were completed. Under the Qing dynasty, reports of the scientific revolution in Europe began to reach China by way of Jesuit missionaries, foreshadowing centuries of European domination.

THE MING DYNASTY AND THE CULMINATION OF CHINESE SCIENCE

At the beginning of the fourteenth century, the Mongol-led Yuan dynasty was beginning to collapse. During these turbulent and violent times, an impoverished Buddhist monk—angry at the destruction of his temple—joined an uprising force called the Red Turban

Rebellion. This man, Zhu Yuanzhang, would eventually win one of the largest naval battles in history: the Battle of Lake Poyang in 1363. During the battle, hundreds of ships and hundreds of thousands of soldiers used gunpowder weapons to their greatest extent yet. Along with the use of Song-style bombs and fire lances, Yuanzhang's navy won using newer muskets and greater tactical skill. After the rebels burned up the enemy fleet, they were able to expel the Mongol rulers and proclaim a new dynasty: the Ming.

As the Ming dynasty consolidated its rule, many scholars set themselves to the task of compiling and systematizing thousands of years of written knowledge, scientific and otherwise. Between 1403 and 1407 CE, scholars compiled an encyclopedia of more than eleven thousand volumes. Chinese medical traditions were standardized after the publication of Li Shi-Zhen's *Ben Cao Gang Mu* (*Compendium of Materia Medica*), which compiled all known medicinal substances in a single book. Other important works were compilations of classics of literature, history, and mechanical engineering. This period of consolidation did not result in any groundbreaking STEM advancements, but it preserved China's long history of discovery for future generations.

Meanwhile, contact with the rest of the world continually increased. China's population expanded due to crops from the New World, such as corn, potatoes, tomatoes, peppers, and sweet potatoes. As a result, the population grew by tens of millions of people, and regions developed their own distinctive cuisine, like pepper-rich Sichuan dishes. In addition,

本草綱目卷之一

序例上

歷代諸家本草

神農本草經

掌禹錫曰舊說本草經三卷神農所作而不經
見漢書藝文志但云醫經七家二百一十六卷
亦無本草之名惟平帝紀云元始五年舉天下
通知方術本草者所在輶軒遣詣京師又樓護傳
稱護少誦醫經本草方術數十萬言本草之名蓋
見於此

韓保昇曰按淮南子云神農嘗百草之滋味一日
而遇七十毒由是醫方興焉蓋上世未著文字師
學相傳謂之本草兩漢以來名醫益眾張機華陀
輩始因古學附以新說厘正舊本刪茸繁蕪增補
遺闕而本草之書備矣

名醫別錄者以李時珍曰神農本草經三品計三百六十五種
應周天之數梁陶弘景復增漢魏以下名醫所用
藥三百六十五種謂之名醫別錄

Chinese tea became a global commodity, which Europeans paid for with enormous amounts of silver, shipped from the Americas.

On the eve of Europe's Age of Exploration, Ming China also enjoyed a final bout of naval supremacy. In 1405, China's greatest admiral—Sheng He—began leading enormous fleets of treasure ships along the Indian Ocean sea route. These demonstrations were intended as displays of force; at close to 200 feet (60 m) long and in fleets of a dozen or more, Sheng He's voyages showed the surrounding world the ongoing richness and power of Imperial China. They also brought back diplomats and exotic animals in order to learn more about other cultures. Unlike European explorers, these Chinese missions had no interest in conquest. Mysteriously, after thirty years of voyages, they were brought to a sudden close. The ships were dismantled, and China withdrew from further exploration.

THE *BEN CAO GANG MU* STANDARDIZES CHINESE MEDICINE

In 1578, a country doctor named Li Shi-Zhen completed the *Ben Cao Gang Mu*, the most important textbook in the history of traditional Chinese medicine. Based on Taoist principles, it served as an encyclopedia of every

(continued on the next page)

(continued from the previous page)

known item used in medicine. Along with herbs—the use of which appears in all traditional medicines—the *Ben Cao Gang Mu* includes entries for mythical items, like dragon bone. This book, like much of traditional Chinese medicine, is an unusual combination of legend, genuine science, and deeply rooted cultural beliefs.

The unusual nature of this classic text raises the question: how does Chinese medicine fit into the larger history of medicine? Unlike the other great Chinese inventions, traditional Chinese medicine has not been as widely adopted. Techniques used in

A modern doctor of traditional Chinese medicine is shown here applying moxibustion to a patient. This practice burns herbal remedies near the skin to change the flow of qi in the body.

traditional Chinese medicine, such as acupuncture, diagnosis of illness using the pulse, and moxibustion (heat therapy using burning herbs), have not been proven effective when examined in modern scientific trials. The administration of medical care according to different forms of qi has also not translated into scientific practice.

However, Chinese medicine is still a valuable piece of China's STEM history. Chinese doctors developed one of the earliest precursors to the smallpox vaccine. They found that by grinding smallpox scabs into a powder and inhaling it by nose, the exposure would prevent future threats from the deadly disease. This practice, widespread during the Ming dynasty, was significantly more advanced than in Europe, where inoculation was more painful and less effective. In the present day, acupuncture is practiced alongside standard medicine in some hospitals, suggesting that the final chapter on traditional Chinese medicine has not yet been written.

THE QING DYNASTY AND THE DOMINANCE OF EUROPEAN SCIENCE

It is fitting that the final Chinese dynasty was established by yet another outside conquest, as China would remain under the shadow of other powers for the final centuries of its empire. Hong Taiji, a lord from modern-day Manchuria, invaded the Ming dynasty from the north. Taking advantage of a peasant rebellion occurring at the same time, Hong managed to conquer the capital of Beijing, proclaiming the beginning of the Qing dynasty in 1644 CE.

Though regionally powerful, the Qing dynasty had been surpassed by the advances in Europe during the concurrent scientific revolution. Having absorbed the inventions and findings of China, India, Persia, and the Arab world, European scientists began making discoveries of their own—and thanks to the curiosity of one Qing emperor, these findings started making their way to China.

Starting in the sixteenth century CE, China began receiving visits from Jesuits, members of a Catholic organization called the Society of Jesus. Though the Jesuits' goal was to convert the Chinese to Christianity, their policy was less forceful than other missionary organizations. Instead, they pursued cultural exchanges, especially in science. Emperor Kangxi, who ruled from 1661 to 1722 CE, was interested in science and invited the priests to join his court. The Jesuits first found favor by curing Kangxi's malaria with quinine, but they primarily advised the emperor on subjects the Chinese had pioneered centuries earlier: astronomy, mathematics, and gunpowder weapons.

Unfortunately, cultural conflicts would doom the relationship between the Jesuits and the Chinese. The priests encouraged many Chinese scholars to destroy their pagan books and melt down their mechanical devices, resulting in the loss of many treasures of Chinese intellectual history. The partnership

In the early years of Kangxi's long and successful reign, he invited visiting Jesuits to join the court and share their scientific knowledge. Unfortunately, religious disputes cut short this exchange.

permanently soured when Qing officials began to forbid the Jesuits from participating in Confucian rituals. In the end, the Qing dynasty cut off contact with Christian missionaries.

Though the exchange of ideas between the Jesuits and the Qing dynasty ended with a severing of ties, classical Chinese culture had another unexpected contribution to European thought. As traveling Jesuits began returning to Europe from China, they brought the ideas of Confucius back with them. There, Confucian ideas influenced a number of important European thinkers. The philosopher Gottfried Wilhelm Leibniz was a reader of Confucius, as were Enlightenment philosophers who yearned for a model of righteous rule that was fitting in the modern world. The most fruitful engagement was from French economist François Quesnay. Inspired by the concept of wu wei, he translated these ideas into French as laissez-faire, which has been interpreted to mean "let (the people) do as they choose." Using this concept, Quesnay argued that governments should not involve themselves in the economy. Laissez-faire became the foundation of free-market economics, thanks to the unexpected travels of China's greatest philosopher.

Though ancient Chinese thought made its way around Europe—and the world—during the Qing dynasty, China would not return to scientific and industrial power until the end of the twentieth century. Brought under the economic and military influence of the British Empire, China would remain stagnant and divided by internal conflicts. For a long time, even the great inventions of China would be forgotten, the credit for them taken by Europeans and other growing world powers. Though ancient traditions had been instrumental in the unbelievable advancements in Chinese STEM, the Central Kingdom was now weighed down by restrictions, paving the way for Europe's rise.

This situation, however, is fast changing in the twenty-first century. China is reviving its industry and placing new emphasis on scientific advances, all while looking back to its own past for inspiration. Though the future of Chinese STEM may not rely on the Mandate of Heaven, Confucius, and Taoism, one thing is clear: China is willing to learn from its past to build a future of innovation. STEM played a major role in China's traditional self-identity, as it likely will well into the future.

François Quesnay, an eighteenth-century French economist and political scientist, adopted many of Confucius's ideas in his theories and writing.

TIMELINE

Sixteenth century BCE The first recorded Chinese dynasty, the Shang, is established.

1046 BCE The Zhou dynasty overtakes the Shang and proclaims the first Mandate of Heaven.

551 BCE Confucius, China's most important philosopher, is born during the Spring and Autumn periods.

221 BCE The Qin dynasty unifies the independent warring states, establishing Imperial China. Construction commences on the Great Wall of China.

206 BCE Emperor Gaozu establishes the Han dynasty, often seen as the golden age of Chinese civilization.

581 CE The Sui dynasty is established, ending a second lengthy period of instability. Older canals are connected into the Grand Canal.

618 CE The Tang dynasty is established, beginning a period of urbanization in China.

868 CE   The *Diamond Sutra*, a Buddhist text, is the first known complete printed book.

960 CE   The Song dynasty is established and begins to dominate Indian Ocean trade.

1206 CE   Temujin, a Mongol warrior, is proclaimed Genghis Khan, leader of all Mongols. He begins conquering the surrounding areas, including parts of China.

1271 CE   Kublai Khan, grandson of Genghis Khan, founds the Yuan dynasty in the areas of China he captured. His conquest of China is completed in 1279.

1298 CE   The earliest dated gun is manufactured, though guns had been used in warfare much earlier.

1368 CE   Zhu Yuanzhang, a former Buddhist monk, defeats the Mongols in an armed rebellion and proclaims himself emperor of the new Ming dynasty. The Ming are the last ethnic Chinese dynasty.

1405 CE   Chinese admiral Zheng He embarks on the first of seven voyages in his great fleet of treasure ships.

1582 CE   Matteo Ricci, a Jesuit priest, arrives at the Portuguese colony of Macau. His reports of Chinese culture begin a period of intellectual exchange between the Jesuits and the Chinese.

1644 CE   The Qing dynasty conquers China. It is the last dynasty to rule China, before the Imperial system was ended by the short-lived Republic of China in 1912.

GLOSSARY

acupuncture A branch of traditional Chinese medicine that treats illness by inserting tiny needles at strategic points in the body.

alchemy A precursor to chemistry that was widely practiced in the Middle Ages; especially interested in the properties of matter.

algebra A branch of mathematics focused on solving for unknown quantities, represented with symbols.

armillary sphere A device constructed to represent a model of the universe, typically including the Earth, sun, stars, and moon.

astrology A nonscientific interpretation of astronomical information; used to identify possible future omens.

astronomy The systematic observation of phenomena in the night sky.

cavalry A military outfit riding on horseback; an especially important asset in historical warfare.

civil engineering A branch of engineering that focuses on the construction of public works, especially roads, bridges, and buildings.

Confucianism A philosophy derived from the teachings of Confucius, who made recommendations for how to create a virtuous society.

hydraulic engineering A branch of engineering that focuses on constructing artificial waterways, redirecting rivers, and building dams.

Jesuit A member of the Society of Jesus, a Catholic missionary organization founded by Ignatius of Loyola in 1534.

junk A traditional Chinese sailing ship, used in both river and sea travel.

kiln An oven in which ceramics are fired in order to harden them for practical use.

Legalism A Chinese political philosophy that believed in strict, precise punishments for all crimes as a way to ensure order.

Mandate of Heaven The traditional Chinese belief that dynasties rise and fall due to the virtue of their leaders.

metallurgy The practice of refining and working metals into tools and weapons, involving high heat and technical skill.

monsoon A wind pattern in the Indian Ocean that seasonally changes directions; used for Indian Ocean travel.

polymath Somebody who is skilled in more than one scientific or intellectual discipline, i.e. mathematics and physics.

polynomial A type of algebraic problem with multiple terms at more than one power.

porcelain A type of pottery that is fired at high temperatures, resulting in an especially strong material.

steppe A Eurasian biome characterized by grasslands; frequently settled by nomadic populations.

stirrups Devices attached to the sides of a saddle, allowing a horse rider to easily stabilize.

Taoism A Chinese religion that is interested in the secret workings of nature.

trigonometry A branch of mathematics based in the properties of angles and their relationship with sides of a triangle.

FOR MORE INFORMATION

Asian Politics and History Association
1840 Michael Faraday Drive, Suite 100
Reston, VA 20190
(571) 526-4777
Website: http://www.aphadc.org
The Asian Politics and History Association has a free
    online publication, as well as free print journals
    available on request.

Canada Science and Technology Museum
1867 St. Laurent Boulevard
Ottawa, ON K1G 5A3
Canada
(866) 442-4416
Website: https://ingeniumcanada.org/cstm
Facebook: @IngeniumCa
Instagram: @IngeniumCanada
Twitter: @SciTechMuseum
The Canada Science and Technology Museum has
    online interactive displays, digital collections to
    explore, and upcoming exhibition information.

History of Science Society
440 Geddes Hall
University of Notre Dame
Notre Dame, IN 46556
(574) 631-1194
Website: https://hssonline.org
Facebook: @HistoryOfScienceSociety
Twitter: @hssonline

The History of Science Society is one of the oldest organizations dedicated to the history of science. Along with access to scholarly databases, it supports digital history projects.

International Institute for Asian Studies
Rapenburg 59
2311 GJ Leiden
Netherlands
+31-71-5272227
Website: https://iias.asia
Twitter: @AsianStudies
The International Institute for Asian Studies has a wide range of research goals, including current politics and older history. Its website includes pages on the history of science in Asia.

Needham Research Institute
8 Sylvester Road
Cambridge CB3 9AF
England
+44-(0)1223 311545
Website: http://www.nri.cam.ac.uk
Twitter: @NeedhamResearch
The Needham Research Institute is one of the most prestigious organizations studying the history of science in China. Its website includes introductory materials and recent publications.

University of Alberta China Institute
203 Telus Centre
87 Avenue & 111 Street
Edmonton, AB T6G 2R1
Canada
(780) 492-1263
Website: https://www.ualberta.ca/china-institute
Twitter: @UalbertaChina
The China Institute conducts events and research
    on current events in China, as well as hosting a
    podcast in English and Chinese.

FOR FURTHER READING

Bardoe, Cheryle, and the Field Museum. *China: A History*. New York, NY: Abrams Books for Young Readers, 2018.

Brezina, Corona. *Zheng He: China's Greatest Explorer, Mariner, and Navigator*. New York, NY: Rosen Publishing, 2017.

Culp, Jennifer. *Ancient Chinese Technology*. New York, NY: Rosen Publishing, 2017.

Dreier, David L. *The Yuan Dynasty*. New York, NY: Rosen Publishing, 2017.

Faust, Daniel R. *The Rise and Fall of the Ming Dynasty*. New York, NY: Rosen Publishing, 2017.

Frankopan, Peter, and Neil Packer. *The Silk Roads: A New History of the World*. New York, NY: Bloomsbury Children's Books, 2018.

Liu-Perkins, Christine. *At Home in Her Tomb: Lady Dai and the Ancient Chinese Treasures of Mawangdui*. Watertown, MA: Charlesbridge, 2014.

Randolph, Joanne. *Living and Working in Ancient China*. New York, NY: Enslow, 2018.

Vietze, Andrew. *Kublai Khan: Emperor of China*. New York, NY: Rosen Publishing, 2017.

BIBLIOGRAPHY

Andrade, Tonio. *The Gunpowder Age: China, Military Innovation, and the Rise of the West in World History*. Princeton, NJ: Princeton University Press, 2016.

Benjamin, Craig. *Empires of Ancient Eurasia: The First Silk Roads Era, 100 BCE–250 CE*. Cambridge, UK: Cambridge University Press, 2018.

Benn, Charles. *Daily Life in Traditional China: The Tang Dynasty*. Westport, CT: Greenwood Press, 2002.

Bol, Peter K. *Neo-Confucianism in History*. Cambridge, MA: Harvard University Press, 2008.

Clarke, J. J. *Oriental Enlightenment: The Encounter Between Asian and Western Thought*. London, UK: Routledge, 1997.

Ebrey, Patricia, and Anne Walthall. *East Asia: A Cultural, Social, and Political History*. Boston, MA: Wadsworth, 2014.

Feng, Linda Rui. *City of Marvel and Transformation: Chang'an and Narratives of Experience in Tang Dynasty China*. Honolulu, HI: University of Hawai'i Press, 2015.

Hessler, Peter. *Oracle Bones: A Journey Between China's Past and Present*. New York, NY: HarperCollins e-Books, 2014.

Holcombe, Charles. *The Genesis of East Asia: 221 B.C.–A.D. 907*. Honolulu, HI: University of Hawai'i Press, 2001.

Katz, Victor J. *A History of Mathematics: An Introduction*. Boston, MA: Pearson, 2008.

Keightley, David N. *These Bones Shall Rise Again: Selected Writings on Early China*. Edited by Henry

Rosemont Jr. Albany, NY: State University of New York Press, 2014.

Liu, Xinru. *The Silk Road in World History*. Oxford, UK: Oxford University Press, 2010.

Loewe, Michael, and Edward L. Shaughnessy, eds. *The Cambridge History of Ancient China: From the Origins of Civilization to 221 B.C.* Cambridge, UK: Cambridge University Press, 1999.

Lu, Xun. "Confucius in Modern China." In *Jottings under Lamplight*, 183–189. Cambridge, MA: Harvard University Press, 2017.

Lu, Yongxiang, ed. *A History of Chinese Science and Technology*. Heidelberg, Germany: Springer, 2015.

Nappi, Carla. *The Monkey and the Inkpot: Natural History and Its Transformations in Early Modern China*. Cambridge, MA: Harvard University Press, 2009.

Needham, Joseph, et al., eds. *Science and Civilization in China*. Cambridge, UK: Cambridge University Press, 2015.

Sellmann, James D. *Timing and Rulership in "Master Lü's Spring and Autumn Annals (Lüshi Chunqiu)."* Albany, NY: State University of New York Press, 2002.

Temple, Robert. *The Genius of China: 3,000 Years of Science, Discovery, and Invention*. New York, NY: Simon and Schuster, 1986.

Twitchett, Denis, and John K. Fairbank, eds. *The Cambridge History of China*. Cambridge, UK: Cambridge University Press, 2019.

Von Glahn, Richard. *The Economic History of China: From Antiquity to the Nineteenth Century*. Cambridge, UK: Cambridge University Press, 2016.

INDEX

ABOUT THE AUTHOR

Michael Hessel-Mial has a PhD in comparative literature from Emory University, where he specialized in the relationship between literature and the history of science. Along with publishing broadly in poetry and literary studies, he has written or edited more than a dozen books, including a digital poetry anthology and several titles for New York Times Educational Publishing, an imprint of Rosen Publishing. Hessel-Mial traveled to China for the first time in 2016 and has been especially interested in China ever since. He currently teaches the history of thought at the Kansas City Art Institute.

PHOTO CREDITS

Cover Raymond Shi/EyeEm/Getty Images; pp. 5, 29 Robert Kawka/Alamy Stock Photo; pp. 9, 54 Pictures from History /Bridgeman Images; pp. 12, 18 British Library, London, UK /© British Library Board. All Rights Reserved/Bridgeman Images; pp. 14, 65 Christophel Fine Art/Universal Images Group /Getty Images; p. 20 Ashmolean Museum, University of Oxford, UK/Gift of Mr. C. Norris/Bridgeman Images; 22 Alan Copson /Photographer's Choice/Getty Images; p. 26 Science & Society Picture Library/Getty Images; p. 31 The Metropolitan Museum of Art, New York/Purchase, Friends of Asian Art Gifts, 2003. www. metmuseum.org/art/collection/search/72326; p. 35 richcano /iStock/Getty Images;p. 39 De Agostini Picture Library /Getty Images; p. 40 The Metropolitan Museum of Art, New York, Rogers Fund, 1918. www.metmuseum.org/art/collection /search/42476; p. 45 FLHC 62/Alamy Stock Photo; p. 49 Bridgeman Art Library/Getty Images; p. 52 MPI/Archive Photos /Getty Images; p. 58 First edition of Bencao Gangmu, Chinese, 1590. Wellcome Collection. CC BY 4.0; p. 60 nik wheeler /Corbis NX/Getty Images; p. 63 Fine Art/Corbis Historical /Getty Images; cover and interior pages (dark textured background) Midiwaves/Shutterstock.com; interior pages (scroll pattern page borders) Megin/Shutterstock.com, (yellow marbled page borders) Chizhovao/Shutterstock.

Design and Layout: Nicole Russo-Duca; Editor: Siyavush Saidian; Photo researcher: Cindy Reiman